This book belongs to

Steven Hopley

Presented by

Auntie Anne and Uncle Dave

on

March 31, 2002

For my Granddaughters,
Amy and Anna

GOD'S LOVE at EASTER

Joy Morgan Davis ❖ Illustrated by Marion Eldridge

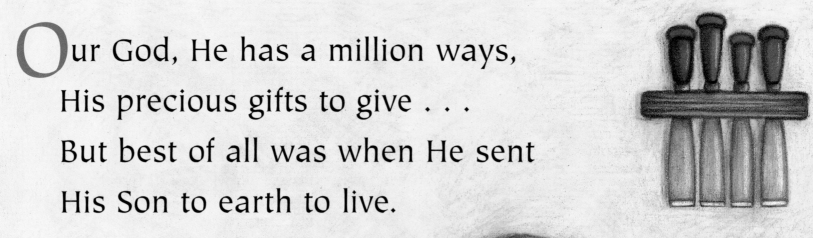

Our God, He has a million ways,
His precious gifts to give . . .
But best of all was when He sent
His Son to earth to live.

As long as Jesus was on earth,
The love of God He told.
That's why He came ... and left His home
Along the streets of gold.

He took the children on His knee,
And taught them how to pray.
He told them that the Father's care
Was with them every day.

He healed the sick of their disease,
And made the blind to see.

He stopped the winds and stayed the waves
Upon a stormy sea.

Yet Jesus knew the time must come
When He would give His life . . .
A sacrifice to save the world
From all its sin and strife.

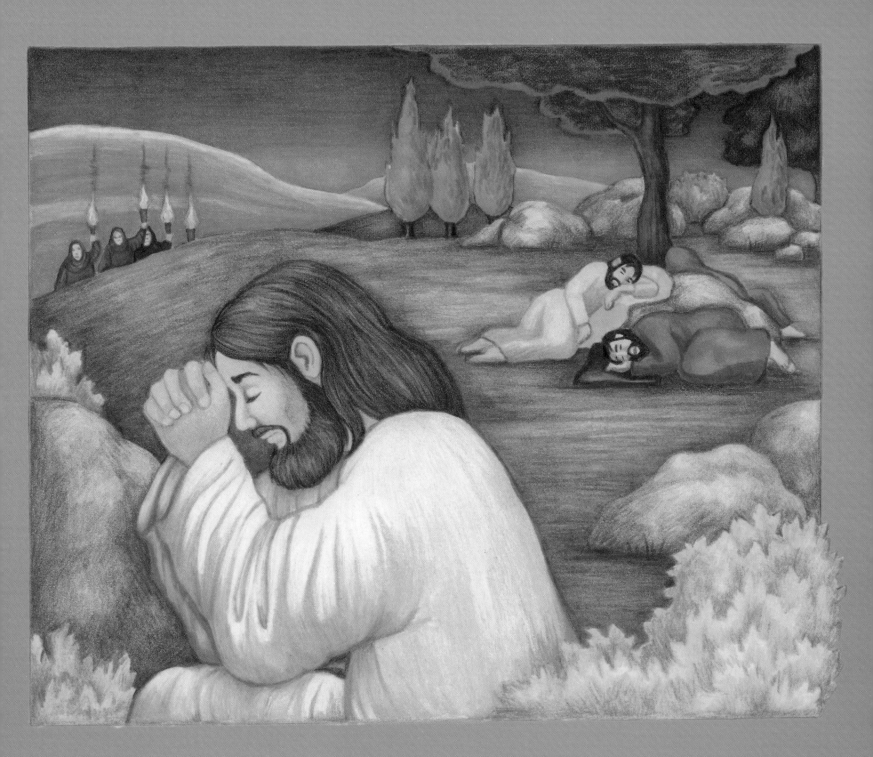

The soldiers took Him to the cross,
And had Him crucified.
It was the saddest day on earth . . .
The day that Jesus died.

Friends laid Him in a garden tomb,
And put in place a stone.
And then with heavy hearts they wept,
To leave Him there alone.

But God performed a miracle
As people cried that night.
God raised His Son! And Jesus walked
From darkness into light.

He went to see those faithful friends—
He let them touch and see,
So they could know He was alive
And we could all believe . . .

He died for us upon a cross—
Our sins are now forgiven.
God claims us as His very own,
And welcomes us to heaven.

And now we show with our own lives,
And share with everyone
That God so dearly loved the world,
He gave His only Son.

And so each year we celebrate
God's love on Easter day . . .

The day when at the garden tomb
The stone was rolled away.

SAINT LOUIS

Text copyright © 2002 Joy Morgan Davis

Illustrations copyright © 2002 Marion Eldridge

Published by Concordia Publishing House, 3558 S. Jefferson Avenue, St. Louis, MO 63118-3968

Manufactured in the United States of America

1   2   3   4   5   6   7   8   9   10   11   10   09   08   07   06   05   04   03   02